vox poetica
inspirations: images & words

collection 3, fall 2011

ISBN 978-1-936373-23-9

© 2011 Unbound Content, LLC. All rights retained by the original authors and artists with the exception of first-time anthology rights to distribute in this collection. These first-time anthology rights are held by Unbound Content, LLC, published as part of the **vox poetica** *inspirations* collections.

All images reprinted here are owned by Gianluca D'Elia, Annmarie Lockhart, and Patti Forehand. Permission for use requests will be forwarded.

vox poetica *inspirations: images & words*
collection 3, fall 2011

With much appreciation to **Gianluca D'Elia**, **Annmarie Lockhart**, and **Patti Forehand** for the photographs that inspired these words, and the **writers** and **readers** who share their talents and passions, who give and take, who are the living expression of artistic community.

table of contents

On the Strand

Scarlett's Lament, by Gianluca D'Elia 9
Painting the Edge, by John Lavan 10
Rail Watching, by Stan Galloway 10
We Read the Same Books, by Annmarie Lockhart 11
The Little Mermaid (Uncensored), by Telly McGaha 12
Shoreline, by Mildred Speidel 14
Scallop and me, by Sarah Endo 15
Shards of Past, by Nick Hawkins 15
Losing Myself in the Rhythm, by Phyllis Johnson 16
That Day, by Jack Daily 17
Impressions by the Sea, by Grace Burns 18
The Birth of Venus, by Ray Sharp 19
Shores of Despair, by Kathryn Tate Jacoby 20
Lithos, by Rae Spencer 21
This Beloved Deep, by Clarissa McFairy 22
Searching, by Christine Tapson 23
The Morning I Stare at the Water for Hours, by Bryan Borland 24
Morning Sun, by Bobbie Troy 25
Help, by Jean McLeod 25
Midweek at the Beach, by Cassie Premo Steele 26
Perspective, by Helen Losse 27
Waves Against the Rocks, by Jeanette Cheezum 27
clawing my way back to the calm, by Lisa Nielsen 28
If, by Patti Forehand 29
Ocean, by Marla Deschenes 30
A Change in the Tides, by Joanna S Lee 31
Sweet Release, by Mark Gooch 32
SeaScape, by Joan McNerney 33

Neptune's Court

Our Poseidon Adventure, by Marla Deschenes 37
I Swim With Fishes, by Nick Hawkins 38
Neptune, by Jeanette Cheezum 39
the flight of Aeneas, by Joanna S Lee 40

Maybe in Ithaca, by Annmarie Lockhart... 41
Fear Not, by Ray Sharp.. 41
Mid-marriage, high tide, by Cassie Premo Steele 42
Untitled, by Stephen Luke 43
Creative Detonation, by Sara Fryd 44
Without a Trace, by Lisa Nielsen 45
Waist Deep, by Nate Spears 46
Rise and Fall of Neptune, by Clarissa McFairy 47
Coming Home, by Jeanette Gallagher 48
Through the Eye of the Fish, by Bobbie Troy 49
Legends, by Mark Gooch 50
Poseidon, by Meg Harris 51
Neptune, by Mildred Speidel 51
Neptune's Coquette, by Joan McNerney 52

Seal Rock

She, by Cassie Premo Steele 57
Sanctured Grace (Pups and Squalls), by Nick Hawkins 58
Family, by Mildred Speidel 59
Little Lessons of Life, by Mark Gooch 60
Dependents, by Jeanette Cheezum 61
Untitled, by Stephen Luke 61
Naiad, by Ray Sharp 62
Hurry! by Joan McNerney 63
Untitled, by Marya Zilberberg 64
Not, by Patti Forehand 64
Dishonor Not Thine Angels, by Clarissa McFairy 65
ladies in waiting, by Lisa Nielsen 66
The Sea Calls Them to Their Skins, by Annmarie Lockhart 67
Deora an Róin (Tears of a Seal), by Joanna S Lee 68

Contributor Bios 71

On the Strand

Photo by Gianluca D'Elia

Scarlett's Lament
By Gianluca D'Elia

Underneath the stars
That dot the indigo sky
Scarlett strolls beneath the harbor lights
She wonders where her husband has gone

As a merchant, he'd travel far away
To lands that were
Mystic
Enchanting
Romantic

When he came back he'd bring exotic treasures
Necklaces and diamond rings
So many rare and unknown things
But no, not this time

He sailed away in his ship, quite a long time ago
Saying farewell to the village
Fulfilling his wanderlust
He slowly pulled out of the harbor
No love this year

Scarlett roams the beach
Her footprints create an endless trail
She builds sandcastles that disappear with the waves
She cries, under the lamps of the harbor
Until the lights turn out

vox poetica

Painting the Edge
By John Lavan

of the sea,
a wet crescent of aqua blue,
fizzes up to a pencil line
dropped from a cobalt sky.

In the marine,
streaks of white bubble
like a lady's hair, floating—but really
air pushed up by moon and water, rock.

Behind, see angled land, grass and stone
and sand and green
corrugated weed and looking down to
boots and hanging ochre hands.

Everything made of water—leveled of course—
a Famous Artist's watercolour.

Rail Watching
By Stan Galloway

From oceanside seats
Gray, wet rocks resist all force
Pleased, looking landward.

We Read the Same Books
By Annmarie Lockhart

There was duck, or was it shrimp tails for calcium?
It was Thai, but it might have been Mexican. The
place was empty, it was crowded, it was early, she
was late. These details came before and after, and
though witty, did not advance the plot. This story,
about him and her, was written in the sand, drawn
in the stars. It caught their laughter up on a surfer's
September waves. It pulled them, naked, away from
rocks and wrecks, into white-green phosphorescent froth.

The first chapter ended with wonder, words, a walk;
its last sentence was a perfect constellation kiss.

vox poetica

The Little Mermaid (Uncensored)
By Telly McGaha

She saw the gentle waves crashing
upon Danish shores, and for once
everything seemed attainable:
life under the sea was overrated,
and everyone knew the seaweed
was greener on the other side
of the coral. So she sprouted
legs and leaped from the crests,
almost drowning for not knowing
how to swim, and partly from being
ecstatic, which is the ruin of most people
in the end, both above and under.

It was not what it seemed, and she realized
life can be cruel and men were fickle. Sure,
she tried the rebound game
after the first prince didn't work out,
but they all came to nothing,
and none were as handsome as him.
Suddenly, life seemed simpler under the sea,
despite its murky, dark depths she might marry
a handsome young merman and make
quite the enviable life for herself. After all,
she was the most desired maid in Kattegat
(though she secretly still hated Kattegat).

So she summoned her evolutionary gift
of phosphorescence and tried to make haste
to Laeso Rende, but hopes, like most things,
were not meant to be, even though her sisters
met her not too far into Oresund, bringing
with them drabskniven, but

already the sea witch was upon them.
She didn't really care:
at this point, she preferred to die for herself
rather than for country, for him, or for love.

The sea witch, of course, asked why
(being sea-provincial it was her nature),
but it was no holds barred and the maid refused
to speak. Instead she said "fuck dat"
and took up the drabskniven and cast it
into her chest, knowing the tide
was high enough to return her:
"Better to wash up and rot in Kobenhavn
than the hell hole of Kattegat," were her
last words, and it outraged her sisters
and especially the sea-witch.
What she didn't say
was such a pretty pearl-encrusted knife
was undeserving of his flesh,
and, to be honest, more suitable for hers,
so vanity still won out in the end.

vox poetica

Shoreline
By Mildred Speidel

I am blue and beautiful
Azure with my white
flowing hair

I see the rocks
They don't disturb me
I lash against them
They seem to come
alive with my touch

They protect me
from hitting the
shoreline

Today the seals
will come
I see them
They will eat
the bounty
that I have brought

I will be back
again and again
I feel your desire
to be touched
with my energy

Scallop and me
By Sarah Endo

at the edge of the salt pond
I hold you
thrilled
to find you
open, revealing
Paul Newman
eyes, billions it seems
fringing your fleshy mantle
but actually dozens
each one electric blue
like a rain
forest butterfly
mesmerized I dangle in a pinkie
you snap shut—tight!
on unsuspecting skin

Shards of Past
By Nick Hawkins

Shards of past.
Here they lie, broken pieces.
For decades dissolve my reputation,
seas wash time and stars watch.
I have no bearing on what I was,
some see me as a stranger of tides,
an ugly remnant of nature's wrath,
but I know the beauty I once adorned.
Pillars of architectural brilliance ...
entrancing sailors of fortune into a port of enrichment.
I'm collapsed, fungi-ridden and unrecognizable today,
survived by the ocean and her century's tales.
My pride is my silence.
And this is me, shards of past.

Losing Myself in the Rhythm
By Phyllis Johnson

Dipping my feet into the water
I feel the ocean's flow,
shades of warm and cool
I lose myself in the rhythm,
it passes by me
like my life.

I sit atop a ledge
jutting out
taunting the waves
that tickle and lick
its craggy ledge.

Foam dances by,
swirls past me,
teasing and tossing
its froth about
as fish dart and dive.

Laughing, I watch them,
losing myself in the
chase below.
The sun, setting now
kisses good bye.

For its work is done.
I raise my legs,
stand up and walk away,
a backwards glance at
rocks, waves and mist.
A seagull flies overhead
shrieking out
a loud goodbye.

That Day
By Jack Daily

We walked on sun sparkled sand
Smiling, thinking,
      holding each other's gaze.
            The hours pushed the tide away.
We laughed, as you cried wet tears
Of joy into my stories.
Our footprints tracing new memories
      along the way,
           it was a witty day that day.

vox poetica

Impressions by the Sea
By Grace Burns

Grandpa stood in wet sand
amongst dead horseshoe crabs and jellyfish
casting out then reeling in
his fishing line to hook new bait.
The fish were hungry but too wily to be caught.

I searched for seashells and driftwood
and presented these gifts to Grandpa.
He gladly accepted these offerings
and gently placed them into the dirty white bucket
where the fish were supposed to go.

Grandpa still visits this beach
fishing pole in hand
and fills the bucket meant for his catch
with treasures from the sea
found by the ghosts of my childhood.

The Birth of Venus
By Ray Sharp

Love was born one starry night at the shore,
not a babe in arms but a woman in full
with skin fair as moonlight, red hair
and artful hands her modest coquetry

as she stood naked in the briny breeze.
He longed to answer the demands of her
small round breasts, to touch the face
of a goddess and hips of an earthly woman,

their gentle bump and sway from the realm
of waves, her eyes sea-foam green.
Love rose on that balmy night, a miraculous
figure dancing on the fluid world

beyond the docks, beyond the rocks,
beyond the pale designs of mere men.

vox poetica

Shores of Despair
By Kathryn Tate Jacoby

It was so very long ago,
but seems as if just yesterday ...

and the sound of the waves upon the rocks
is painful, too painful to contemplate

Too many times he took chances
thinking he was infallible, invincible
racing toward the shore late at night
after the traps were in

hurrying home to her

But this time he played it too close
probably laughing all the way to the bottom ...

It was his way, his life, his identity

Instead of the rush of adrenaline
that gave him reason to do what he did each day,
this time it was his demise

Oh but he went as he would have wanted

And so, though she mourns
she also understands

He couldn't resist

Lithos
By Rae Spencer

In a test of tide and stone
Earth's odds favor tide

Even the moon pulls for it

Adamant siege of surge
And retreat, slosh and roll

Relentless as time

Lapping past this present
Verge, confused headland

Mapped in brine and drift

The savored memory
Of what stood, what stands

Until sifted to sand

Briefly printed mold
Unreliable anchor

Shifting underfoot

Lost between trough
and breaking crest, erased

In eternity's rush and loll

This Beloved Deep
By Clarissa McFairy

Ah, the Deep,
my deep, deep sleep …
Hold back awhile
so I can rest
my late blooming cheek
against this other Deep,
this beloved Deep
that shimmers at my feet

Your stars above,
Mine below!

Quicksilvery
Mermaids of the Deep,
show me how to dance
and dip and glide
on silver spangled wings
in this beloved Deep,
before you sing me
to my deeper sleep

Searching

By Christine Tapson

There's the calm (superficially calm)
And the friendly wave (small but present)
At least it's there. The wave.

The apparent stillness not so still
Look below, look closely
See the storm beneath the surface.

The quiet sea not so quiet.

Who put those rocks there?
Carefully placed. Haphazard. Unmoving.
Eternal rocks in the road.

We have to navigate
Stand on the barricade
Leap toward freedom

Put the hurdles and obstacles behind us
And find what we need.
Or perhaps what we're looking for.

vox poetica

The Morning I Stare at the Water for Hours

By Bryan Borland

I feel kinship with the waves that carried you
to the bank, letting you rest on a thousand
lilied fingertips, wet as the day you were born.

I am in their debt, this matter that blanketed you
like a newborn, that held and rocked you to sleep
in time with the pull of the moon. These bodies

are your cemetery, these streams and gulfs between us,
these tides that returned you to the womb
and brought to an end money, grudge, gravity.

I want to know these things, the great unknowable,
the great inevitable, so I take off my shoes
and socks and wade into the water. The river

has a summer's warmth, far from the wintery lake
of your cold and quiet finale. Life is liquid, the current
through my toes, the minnows around my ankles,

you are dust and mud and memories here, the science
that surrounds me, that circles each moment
and ripples toward the center of everything.

Morning Sun

By Bobbie Troy

the morning sun
cleaved the air
revealing rocks and sea

i stand alone
in the sun
with just your memory

Help

By Jean McLeod

I needed you
but all that was left
were sails
beyond the waves.

vox poetica

Midweek at the Beach
By Cassie Premo Steele

At first it feels endless
the loneliness of the distance
from morning until the end.

No one has died. Nothing is lost.
You still have all your friends.

But the sea sees something deeper.
The waves that rise to greet
you from below. They mirror your

white shadow of longing. How tired you are
of desire. Reaching. Belonging.

Once, when your daughter was a baby,
you were walking over rocks like these,
and you thought, I could drop her.

The mood midweek at the beach is like this.
The temptation of not there.

And then something turns.
The sun, the dock, the tide.
And the ocean floor within you learns

once again how to rise.
Coral, anemone, eel, and more

transform the dark. You feel
the spark. What you could do.
Oh the possibility of you.

It throws itself upon the shore.
Wave after wave. Knocks on the door.

Perspective

By Helen Losse

Standing on the wooden walkway
and leaning against the rail. Salty air
sticks to my skin.

Ocean waves
break against
a pile of dark rocks
near the shore.

Somewhere near the horizon,
a mermaid calls from the water.
At times like this, I feel like a child.

My needs are simple:
Someone to feed me fish.
Someone to bring me wine.
Someone to walk on water.

Waves Against the Rocks

By Jeanette Cheezum

Life is like waves slapping up against the rocks,
sometimes gentle, sometimes fierce.
Undersea life creates and goes forth to produce.
Above sea there is something stronger than
mere humans to keep nature afloat.

Soak up the sun's rays, but hover when the storm
threatens our being. Swim and quiver together
when the perfect mate stops by your side.
Life, earth, and sea are ours for the taking.

clawing my way back to the calm

By Lisa Nielsen

jutting up against me
I was caught between a hard place and
the jagged edges of you

in your manic quest to
dislodge me from my safety net
midnight dreams became a gleaming cape
of a million shards of glass

your hand lamely outstretched
me soaring forward

now
jutting up against me and my jagged edges
is the soft gesture of a wave
pushing me back home

If
By Patti Forehand

If she could hear me
I would tell her
I stood dry-eyed against the rail
that hazy day.
From a plain black box
I gathered, bare-handed, her dusty remains.
My fingernails were too long
and pieces of her lodged underneath them.
I stretched far and leaned well
so some of her ashes would reach the rocks.
I needed just a tiny piece of her close by
safe from the outgoing tides.
If I could hear her
she would tell me
the tide returns everyday
and to remember to use a nail brush.

vox poetica

Ocean

By Marla Deschenes

This is your forgotten childhood
Devoid of magical moments spent
Screaming with laughter in the salty spray.
Missing the sunburned cheeks and dirty fingernails
Of a smaller dreamer's pasts.

This is your forgotten imagination
Smashed smoothly against aging rocks
Swirling helplessly in the drowning foam
Of once pristine beaches now tar-tainted and black
We call home.

This is your remembered failure
Past-playing, mind-numbing scenes of horrors realized
Moments of unwanted glaring spotlight
Now hidden under scars
Nakedly visible.

This is who you will become
The intentions were only to save you from
This graphic gray reality,
From this concrete mecca of electronic waves.
This is you without emotion
Without content
This is you

Without the sea.

A Change in the Tides
By Joanna S Lee

I stand unbowed,
shading my eyes from the rays
of a summer's dying, throat
burnt from the tang of too-much
too-fast and without
breath or word or breezy acknowledgment;

the story was written in some other language
than my own and swallowed whole like tequila
with neither pretense nor
lemon, before even there was
regret; before I was found

face-down in a puddle of blue
and of poison; before I touched
my mother's hand, cold on the
morgue slab, for the last time.

When moonlight still tasted sweet and
deceit melted on the tongue like taffy;
before I had yet reckoned
the consequences.

Now from back upon the shore
the ocean sounds wistful,
a slapping against the rocks as if
in remonstrance; she howls.

I stand unbowed before her
wary of each mouthful of hard-won air;
sea-salt has a bitterness
once you've escaped from
drowning.

vox poetica

Sweet Release
By Mark Gooch

Perched on a platform
at the end of the world
surrounded by ridges
denuding the stones

Their sounds are so soothing
melodious, sweet
song of the ages
no voice can compete

He is awed by the sight
of the creator's design
free from hate or delusion
lacking promises, despair

Entering slowly at first
the realm of gray, green, and blue
the warmth envelopes his body
his beating heart is no more

No pain to endure
his soul is at rest
a new home he found
sweet release arrives at last

SeaScape
By Joan McNerney

My mind is an ocean
where swimmers, surfers,
sun worshipers cavort.

Long salty hair
held between
their teeth.
Flourishing
       wild flowered gowns
           streams of silk
              waves of taffeta
                 splashy lace.

They sail through
my watery face
combing my eyes
whispering in my ears.

Alone, under a pointillist sky.
Gulls flying around me.
Black waters touched by
moon of vague prophecy.

Neptune's Court

Photo by Annmarie Lockhart

Our Poseidon Adventure

By Marla Deschenes

We shall shiver before Poseidon on our knees for what we have done.
We have forgotten that we, like the Sea, are but water
And that our mother sustains us with silent loving care
That sometimes is nothing but silent pain.

Poseidon has watched our decline in what we have done to the Sea.
His angry eyes, flashing deep, are those possessed only by a god.
He has watched his companions die.
His waters blackened with the oil stolen from the Earth's breast.

Who will stand up for the humans and the misguided invincibility?
Who will, with wringing hands, face our demise with fearless beating heart?
The only explanations for our pain are greed and luxury
And the carelessness of thinking we are in control.

The Sea will whisper words of forgiveness in Poseidon's ear
but this, with gentle wave, will be the last time she cares for us.
She is beaten and battered from neglect
And Poseidon lies in wait to exact his revenge for what we have wrought.

vox poetica

I Swim With Fishes
By Nick Hawkins

Ascend into the light, free yourself from the constraints of your mind …
I see you swim with fishes.

Indulge me with tides of nature, help me finally let go …
Dive deep and long into waves of pleasure until you can sleep.

Awaken to the ripples of fulfilling thoughts floating into serenity …
Babylon sings from the depths of these linear waters.

Search skies for what might have been or what may be.
Infuse the roads and miles with the aura of life, greeting others on the way.

I come into the light and sit here to see you from a faraway place …
Can I swim with fishes?

My needs were never like yours and my footsteps are in strange sand
yet I breathe with the ease of being free.

Your tides have swamped my incompetencies and
given me hope for understanding.

Lying still I ascend into the light and travel home, smiling.
It is not about rhythm, soul, rhyme, or song. It's about life.

Your strength has given me what I wanted
until the time we say goodbye.

Until then, I swim with your fishes.

Neptune

By Jeanette Cheezum

Neptune was chosen, not his brothers, Apollo or Zeus; to guard the harbor and command the sea. Ancient warriors attempted to trick him, but none could. His job was to calm the waters while mariners prepared to feed their families and stop the dragons that roared and pillaged. The emerald seas were filled with treasure not to be squandered on mere monsters.

Sunlight shone on Neptune's crown, brought seafarers home with bounty to nurture. Mermaids relaxed with pleasure, knowing he'd protect them and not allow mere mortals to steal them for questionable fantasies.

Humans continue to worship him and carry on his legacy. Myth or not his image is majestic.

vox poetica

the flight of Aeneas
By Joanna S Lee

I sing of arms and the man
born to bear them 'gainst
the wrath of wild horses and
the terror of a tortured earth
chained to a bed of storm,
for where Poseidon shakes
his salt-licked mane and pounds
his three-pronged tempest stave, there
no man nor beast nor sea herself
can rest unwearied through the night
and refugees from fire and death
find no respite; strong shoulders
must carry not only the burden
of aging feet, but also the wrath
of aging gods

Maybe in Ithaca
By Annmarie Lockhart

You leave tomorrow.
And so begin my pilgrimages,
daily, to sea-edge temple.

I will bring sand-specked gifts,
whispered adorations, devout
requests, for I am weak.

I fear this stony god
of the deep will stand mild
aside and let the storms ride

for envy and want of the
fine man's legs that carry you
off to fight another king's battle.

Fear Not
By Ray Sharp

You know I'd rather
salt-sow the rocky fields
of this island of proud men

Than be tide-tugged
by solemn vows and
maelstroms of gods' caprices,

But do not doubt
your down-shore supplications
will be borne to me when

That kelp-clad tyrant
blusters briny winds, as daily
my longing for you increases.

vox poetica

Mid-marriage, high tide
By Cassie Premo Steele

his gray Atlantic swells,
his sad wife sits at a table,
waiting to be served.
there are mockingbirds
and martins and seagulls.
you can't hear them
over the way he yells
at his wife. there is anger
like split seashells
under our steps.
everything ends.
so much we can't
remember. and yet,
we keep walking
along the shore.
we keep getting wet.
sometimes we can
forget. we go swimming.

Untitled
By Stephen Luke

Sights set—

Feet lying on the seaside of humanity,
Of all that is known,

Eyes toward whatever it is that
He decides to discover.

He wavers not,
As of the strongest stone.

While I lazily—
Everything:

Thumb yellowed books, run my fingers through your hair,
Hunker down against the cold air.

I've only found that
Beauty runs through us as sand from our fingers,
And in heaps enough to waste.

All there is to ken,
Deliberate while the other deliberates,
The sands shift, but only over stone.

Creative Detonation
By Sara Fryd

Exotic photographs of images
Of landscapes
Taken by alternates shock me awake
Yet, again …
My brain ceases to comprehend
The meanings of their creative forces
Until …
Appearing as visual jolts of images
That trigger words in patterns
Of fabric, of caramel signs in earth
Of blue sounds in air thru Aspen leaves
Turning gold, then red on arms of
Black striped white bark
Reaching for the sky with empty hands
French lace colored shallow waves
Sweeping in from the calm cashmere ocean
At dusk …
A gold cotton candy sky
Filled with sugary blush clouds
Of photographers' souls
Taken another time, another place
Touch my heart, my soul, my mind
Then seep through my fingers
On to paper, then into thin air

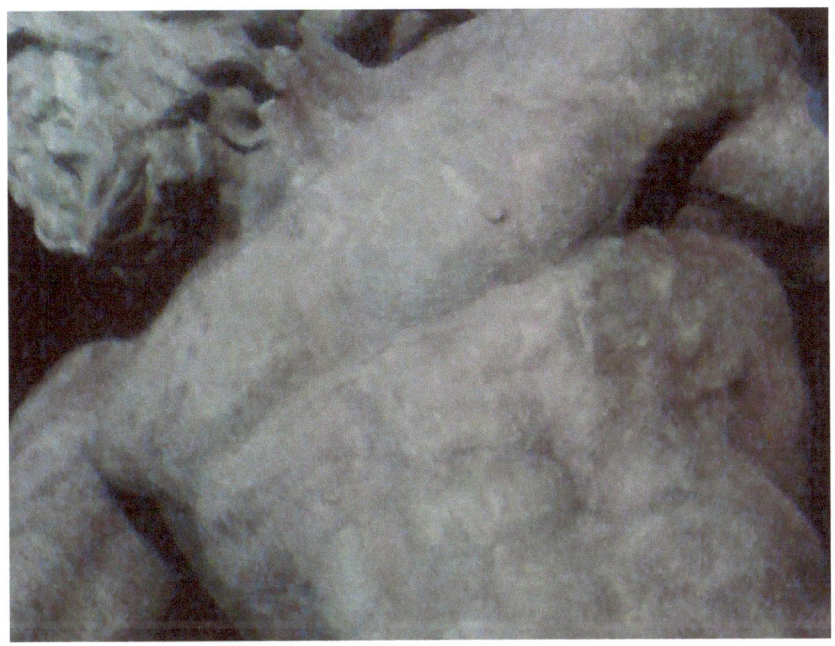

Without a Trace
By Lisa Nielsen

I tried to moisten those indelible pecs
with warm wet kisses
but your stony resolve
would have none of it

It was an exercise in futility, really
did I think it was possible
to buff up those rough edges
like some crazy sander
on a mission to smooth out the world?

Instead I am clawing my way out
of a synapse of seaweed and salty tears
the taste of you stinging my lips
on the familiar highway home

vox poetica

Waist Deep
By Nate Spears

Waist deep in this sea of life
All I have is my staff
I ponder as I choose my path
Atlantic or Pacific
Which way is terrific?
Swallowed up in this sea, I begin to be
Waist deep, water over my knees
Surrounded by millions of fish
Which one do I pick?
I need a keeper
In this ocean I seek her
My staff in hand
I'm a leader
Drowning in this sea I'm in.

Rise and Fall of Neptune
By Clarissa McFairy

Some fig leaf you are wearing,
Neptune!
Is this quilted covering
your quest for quietude
after a night of bliss
on the heaving ocean bed?

Look as thunderous as you like,
God of Storms,
and Earthquakes too?
You are not god of Me,
but a man, who trembles
at each ripple and satin touch

of my sapphire negligee.
I am the Sea,
who swishes and sways
and sweeps you into the deep
where waves of passion
rock you to your sleep.

So quit grandstanding there,
granite-faced "god."
I have seen you and your trident
tumble from your rocky reef,
and know that you are human
under the fancy fig leaf.

vox poetica

Coming Home
By Jeanette Gallagher

At age ten I arrive from mountains in May
in Virginia Beach at two o'clock in the morning.
My family is met by aroma of honeysuckle and gardenia
blended with sand and salt water
from the vast Atlantic Ocean.

My aunt takes my cousins and me straight to the seaside
for our first view of the ocean.
I am enchanted watching gentle waves of ebb tide
caress the moonlit shore then slowly roll back out to sea,
mesmerized by the undulating rhythm of its song.

I know nothing of Neptune, god of the sea,
yet feel his majesty, his mighty arms encompass me.
I feel a mystical joy and know sublime peace.
Surrounded by a loving divine mystery, I belong.
I have come home.

Through the Eye of the Fish

By Bobbie Troy

majesty is calmed
might is made human
swells are tamed
rocks are softened
when seen
through the eye of the fish

vox poetica

Legends
By Mark Gooch

Era of Gods and their brutal control
Bold Travelers
Searching for lands,
Distant shores with perils unknown

   Raging seas,
   Howling winds
   Sea monsters turn you to stone

     No rest
     No peace
     Mermaids sing their seduction song

        Life was hard
        Love was rare
        Dangers abound
        Only the brave would dare
        Conquer the life of the sea

Poseidon

By Meg Harris

The stars fly
from your fingertips;
the little children
of your netting.
You stoop under
the tender branch
of the sun,
as any father might;
stepping carefully
over treetops,
across canyons,
until you cross the desert,
and leap into the
depths of sea.

Neptune

By Mildred Speidel

For centuries I lay at the
bottom of the ocean floor
waiting to be found.

My powers gone, yet I
longed for someone to
find my likeness, to
bring it ashore.

Would the masses know
me now? Would they
bring sacrifices anymore?

Will I be made a fool of
in the pages of history?
Remember my deeds:

I stirred the oceans,
I caused the earth to
shake, I ruled the seas,
storms came on demand

I am Neptune! Son of
Saturn and Ops!
Never forget that!
Never!

vox poetica

Neptune's Coquette

By Joan McNerney

My toes throb over
hard pebbles. Waters slip
over slim ankles. Should I stand
shivering or go swim?
Lose my footprint?

Off I run, falling over myself
a mug of salty cider. This
wave an insecure bed.
Seaweed pillow. Carried by
moon to an abyss.

The floor of my mansion is
not tidy. I shall have sponges
for lunch. Ride with seahorses
perhaps.

On the far shore, my gigantic lover
smiles, kisses of surf. We thread
soft waters while sunshine
dresses us in golden sequins.

Seal Rock

Photo by Patti Forehand

She

By Cassie Premo Steele

Years before she was born, I dreamt of seals
on rocks, the surf below, I did not know
what it meant to be a mother, I thought

it might have something to do with crash
of waves and froth below and the height
of falling into what we do not know

but I did not see the soft brown pelt
surrounding all of this, how every step
your body makes is also chased by her

skin, and no matter how thin you try
to say it is, the fur is there, the wet,
the warmth, the curve of her against

your earth. You were a she before her
birth, now you are mother ever after
and it is she who is she. She is she.

Sanctured Grace
(Pups and Squalls)
By Nick Hawkins

Lazing by nothing,
pondering even less,
matters of no consequence seem consequent.
Words suddenly mean less than life ...
I wonder where they would be without my hidden beauty.

Sitting in silence,
staring quiet,
ssssh! There's an absolute in not giving.
I love remote clear air, blue sea, and empty sky,
this is where I'll remain for at least a while.

Lying still, stagnant in the transient state of now,
unseen by millions and yet impressioned to the few,
keeping leather from the willow is to keep what's mine ...
is to realize someone wants something
now I don't want to give anymore.

Sleeping peace amongst pups and squalls,
I know nothing of my wards, I care less for my suitors,
awake in the knowledge I cost less than a smile,
but this is where I'll remain in sanctured grace.

Family

By Mildred Speidel

We huddle together, we share storms
that lash at our house of stone
We cry, we hold each other

We rebound quickly, Father in the lead
We fish
We eat as a family, sharing

We bask in the California sun
Some humans envy us for that
Oh well, such is life, it's a sealed deal

vox poetica

Little Lessons of Life

By Mark Gooch

Slowly Swaying
Sky Blue Water
Dancing around
Emerald green
Covered rocks

Mother and children
Enjoying the moment
Safe and secure
From storms, hunger, turmoil

Tribute for all
A small reminder indeed
You don't need money or gold
To demonstrate your love

Sharing your time
Will reap great rewards
Memories that will last your life
And create a bond for lifetimes more.

Dependents
By Jeanette Cheezum

Children frolicking on the rocks, waves splashing about them. The sun nurtures while waiting for their mother to feed their needs … no matter what they are.

My camera loves them, black, sleek, and adorable. Would she mind if I wait? Hoping to capture the essence of her return?

I'll sit, I'll bide my time. The proof of a mother's love will once again delight my soul.

Untitled
By Stephen Luke

Up and out of the blue-black water,
She appeared from nowhere, like a shadow from the night.

And in the instant that she materialized,
I saw how much stays undiscovered.
But I sat and awe wandered off.
I began to wonder, questioning the water,
Not showing me before. What other wonders
There remained in the black, thick sea?

I sat with regret
As she sank, deeper I suspect,
Into that dark, heavy world
of risk and ocean alone.

Naiad

By Ray Sharp

She liked to take off her clothes
in the sun-kissed alpine meadows
by the shallow mountain tarns
whenever there was a chance
to slip naked into cool waters.
I remember her rising from blue
and walking straight toward me
as I watched the water stream
down her smooth brown skin
and sleek rounded form and
I said you are made for swimming
like a dolphin or a seal
which she did not hear
quite the way I intended.

Hurry!
By Joan McNerney

Let's stand and sun like salty seals
touching mud with all our toes.
One big wave can push us over
laughing tumbling in the brine.

We'll dive in ocean hiss swish
riding with bluewhales, bluewaves.
Brush of foam and windy ripples
sunbeams chasing quicksilver fish.

Floating through our shining world
fragrant clouds, feathery clouds.
We weave one arm after another
wearing bracelets of watery pearl.

vox poetica

Untitled
By Marya Zilberberg

Beyond ancient cairn my perch
Clear blue beckons
Warmly inviting
Chilling dark depths
Draw me to their mystery
Magnetize my reckless
Desire for
What if?

Not
By Patti Forehand

Maybe
it's not always
supposed to be easy
maybe forced is the way
hidden meanings and seals on rocks
evoking joy and sadness
envy and elation sitting side by side
for a reason
or not
with eyes contemplative
mine
not theirs

Dishonor Not Thine Angels

By Clarissa McFairy

Seals know how to seal time
in warmth and love
To be in the moment,
like a love letter
in an envelope
sealed with a kiss

Those who club them
are clubbing a pact,
a silent communion
between us and the angels
a holy tryst
to honour life

They are clubbing
every trusting smile
of every baby
born to every mother
The ocean shall not wash
the blood from their hands

ladies in waiting
By Lisa Nielsen

is purgatory always this cold
and clammy
or is there a sweet warm abyss
I can slip into
while watchful of the lingerers

we are the huddled masses waiting our turn with you

I bide my time with chatter
mold has grown
and waiting has brought revulsion
(as it always does)
but I do it anyway, laying out with the well-greased,
the glistening, wishing for that whisper

I thought you, under my skin
was exactly what I wanted

I am off to the side now
burrowing my head in the mossy memory
you,
splitting me down the middle
one half held back
the other half willing

The Sea Calls Them to Their Skins
By Annmarie Lockhart

He left. She spilled seven salty tears into
the sullen sea. The moody crash of
high-tide brine kissed her ankles.
And a man stood up, stripped off his
skin, and carried her home.

Happiness held them in a seven-year hold.
Until she awoke to the queasy quiet of
the seven-star night. In its paper-thin
light her man dressed himself and their
two boys in long-hidden skins.

They swam through the sickly green seaweed.
The keening was the rending of her heart,
her womb, that tomb, suddenly bereft, hollow.
Seven years calm, her seas now stormed the
crash of the left behind.

They left. She spilled no tears into the greedy
sea. Now she chases the seventh-cycle light
when her loves return to the hulking rocks
and sing their selkie song of devotions divided
on land by the jealous sea.

vox poetica

Deora an Róin
(Tears of a Seal)

By Joanna S Lee

I've been searching everywhere,

pride an empty sack I carry
slung over one shoulder like
a hunter's bounty, clambering
between rocks the slippery snot-
green of the North Atlantic's wistful
shallows as they long for the sun
and for the jewel-like
aquamarines of summer.

Everywhere.

Hearth and husband only
twilit memories on the steel-
crusted days when the
sea sings in my blood
roaring with an unutterable
ache, and I pace the
gray tangled beaches in loneliness.

Everywhere.

Even unto the seventh wave,
past where these
pale uncouth legs
can yet clutch land,
to where my shivery lungs

cease their heave and ho
and the bright tresses
down this skinless back
shine like pale gold
silk as they sink
into the depths of my
once-home;

though banished without
that with which I left it,
I may at least return to die.

My last
thoughts carry with them
the answer this mutinous
stranger's body could not
find; released beneath the blushing
waters and borne up
with the sea-foam to burst
into understanding where
worlds meet and breakers roll,
they murmur a final lament
to wash up on the shore:

My lover, my protector,
my life, you
stole it from me.

The Contributors

Bryan Borland is the author of *My Life as Adam*, 1 of only 5 collections of poetry included on the American Library Association's Over the Rainbow list of noteworthy LGBT-themed books of 2010. He is the editor of *Assaracus*, the only print journal in the world dedicated exclusively to gay male poets. Keep up with Bryan at bryanborland.com.

Grace Burns lives in New Jersey and is the mother of 2 children. She is an automation and validation engineer, technical writer, mobile DJ, and creative writer. She's also very tired.

Jeanette Cheezum's work has been published online and in print and in 15 anthologies, 3 of which have made *The New York Times* Best Sellers list. She has been awarded the Helium Network's Premium Writer's Badge, Bronze Creative Writing Award, and a Marketplace Writers Award. Jeanette is the editor of *Cavalcade of Stars*.

Jack Daily is a writer and photographer. Born in Birmingham AL, he has lived and worked in Miami and Washington DC in the medical and space industries. He is a member of the Alexandria Art League, the Photography Club of Culpeper, and the Windmore Foundation of the Arts. His photos have appeared in gallery and juried art shows and his writing was published in *Images in Ink* (Windmore Foundation of the Arts, Culpeper VA, 2010) and *City Streets, Off Road, and Through Doors*.

Gianluca D'Elia is an aspiring writer, musician, and photographer. He is also a varsity swimmer. He is currently a sophomore in high school and he lives in New Jersey. His work has appeared at *Caper Literary Journal* and *vox poetica*.

Marla Deschenes writes from her punk rock hideout in suburban Enfield CT, where she is not-so-secretly disguised as a wife, stepmom, and doggie mom. She is currently working on a new zine called That Weird Artist Chick. Her work has been published at *vox poetica* and *SPARK*. She hopes to complete a chapbook of her poetry before the end of 2011.

Sarah Endo lives with her family in Massachusetts. Her poems have appeared online at *Literary Mama* and *vox poetica*.

Patti Forehand is from the Hampton Roads area of Virginia. She is an occasional poet, taking the turtle's approach to memoir writing.

Sara Fryd harbored a secret passion for writing for many years. She would write late at night after selling F-16 ejection seats by day. Born in Tashkent, Uzbekistan, raised in Munich, Sara now lives in Tucson AZ and writes all day long as the mood strikes. Her published books are *What if only one child remained? Woodruff the Chili Dog, The Coincidental Cricket,* and *You Meet No Strangers*.

Jeanette Gallagher moved to Virginia Beach at 10 and grew up in a family-run ocean-front hotel. A retired therapist, she worked at Tidewater Psychiatric Institution and Center of Behavioral Medicine. She is a member of the Albright Poets and Hampton Roads Writers.

Stan Galloway teaches writing and literature at Bridgewater College in the Shenandoah Valley of Virginia. He has had more than 50 poems published at *Red Booth Review, Loch Raven Review, Eunoia Review, Contemporary World Literature, Broad River Review, Boston Literary Review, vox poetica*, and others print and online journals. He has also written a book of literary criticism, *The Teenage Tarzan*.

Mark Gooch is business manager of a medium-sized company in Michigan, where he lives in the rural setting of Clio. He believes writing and reading poetry is the true fountain of youth and suggests everyone take a sip.

Meg Harris is a graduate of Vermont College of Fine Arts. She teaches literature, writing, poetry, critical thinking, and English as a second language. Her short stories, essays, and poems have appeared at *The Whistling Fire, Whiskey Island Magazine, The Cafe Review, Upstreet II, Willows Wept Review,* and other print and online journals. She spends winters in New England with her large family and summers in in a cottage in Southwestern Pennsylvania. Read her blog: bluemoonnortheast.blogspot.com.

Nick Hawkins is from Southern England and writes from a place of image and life. He loves the call of the muse and still believes poetry is born rather than created. He dedicates his work to those he loves, particularly Michael and Amanda Woodhouse, who have shown that true love and courage enable us to climb the highest peaks.

Kathryn Tate Jacoby hails from northern Ohio but proudly calls herself a damn Yankee after 23 years of living in Virginia. She writes about life: "joys, disappointments, the personal growth that inevitably follows." Published in newspapers, anthologies, *The Who's Who of New Poets*, and online literary journals, she is working on her first collection of poetry and photography.

Phyllis Johnson is a poet, author, and photojournalist from Virginia. She has 4 poetry books to her credit, one of which is *Being Frank with Anne,* based on Anne Frank's diary. Her most recent publication is a YA suspense novel, inkBLOT, written with Nancy Naigle. You can read more about her at phyllisjohnson.net.

John Lavan is a poet living in the UK who practices writing at least 1 poem a day. His passion is words and working through them to feeling. His family is his inspiration.

Joanna S Lee lives in Richmond VA, where she spends her free time searching the riverbanks for unborn poetry. Her first book, *the somersaults I did as I fell*, was released in 2009. Her work has been featured recently in litmags such as *Prick of the Spindle* and *Black Fox*, with forthcoming pieces in *Right Hand Pointing* and *qarrtsiluni*. She writes (semi-)regularly at the-tenth-muse.com.

Annmarie Lockhart is the founding editor of *vox poetica* and the founder of unbound CONTENT. She has been reading and writing poetry since she could read and write.

Helen Losse is the author of 2 full-length poetry books, *Seriously Dangerous* (Main Street Rag, 2011) and *Better With Friends* (Rank Stranger Press, 2009) and 2 chapbooks. She has recent poetry publications in *Main Street Rag, Iodine Poetry Review, Wild Goose Poetry Review, The Pedestal Magazine, ken*again, Referential Magazine*, and Georgann Eubanks' *Literary Trails of the North Carolina Piedmont*. She lives in Winston-Salem NC and is the poetry editor for *The Dead Mule School of Southern LIterature*.

Stephen Luke is a writing enthusiast who enjoys copying his favorite poems onto the sidewalks and blacktops of North Jersey for others to discover.

Clarissa McFairy (Clare van der Gaast) is a South African journalist/columnist who lives in Cape Town. Her hobbies are writing short stories and French poetry, some of which she puts to music. She also paints angels and mermaids.

Pushcart Prize nominated **Telly McGaha** resides in Kentucky with his partner and son. His fiction, Patches, was the recipient of the 2007 Hayward Fault Line Competition and was published in *Door Knobs and Body Paint*. His poetry has appeared at *Referential Magazine, Fag Hag: A Scandalous Chapbook of Fabulously Codependent Poetry, Caper Literary Journal, Vwa: Poems for Ayiti, Poets Who Blog,* and *vox poetica*. A collection of his work, known as The Geography of Love, is forthcoming at *Assaracus*, Issue 4.

Jean McLeod's prose and poetry have been published in a number of magazines, periodicals, and journals. She is a Pushcart Prize nominee and her short story "Flowers for Charlie" was made into a movie short subject by Mark Haller-Wade that won Grand Prize at the Hiroshima Film Festival in 1997.

Joan McNerney's poetry has been included in numerous literary magazines such as *Seven Circle Press, Dinner with the Muse, Blueline, 63 channels, Spectrum,* and *3 Bright Spring Press Anthologies*. Four of her books have been published by fine small literary presses.

Lisa Nielsen is a single mom living in Staten Island trying to make sense of how she got there through poetry and random acts of feng shui.

Ray Sharp is a poet of place, if by *place* you mean the Upper Peninsula of Michigan, its forests and cranberry bogs and rocky shores, and the uncharted terrain of the human heart. Ray works in public health by day and dreams in Spanish and French by night.

Nate Spears is a Jacksonville FL native and a published inspirational poet who has more than 100 published poems to his credit. He uses social media and video production to reach out and inspire those in need. Nate began writing at the age of 7 and he was first published 2 years ago. Through hard work and dedication he saw the launch of his debut title, *Inspiration 2 Smile* (unbound CONTENT, 2010). His second collection of poetry is forthcoming at unbound CONTENT.

Mildred Speidel lives in Chesapeake VA and is retired. She has loved poetry for as long as she can remember. She writes what she feels; it works for her.

Rae Spencer is a writer and veterinarian living in Virginia. Her poetry has appeared online and in print, receiving Pushcart Prize nominations in 2009, 2010, and 2011. Her work can be found at raespencer.com.

Cassie Premo Steele's newest collection of poetry, *This is how honey runs* was published by unbound CONTENT in 2010 and her next is forthcoming in the spring of 2012. A frequent contributor to *vox poetica*, she is a Pushcart Prize nominated poet, author of 7 books, and creativity coach who sees clients in person and long distance from her Co-Creating Studio along a little creek in South Carolina. Read her writing and learn about Co-Creating at her web site, www.cassiepremosteele.com.

Christine Tapson was trained as an educational psychologist and remedial therapist, and after working in schools in South Africa, Namibia, and Botswana for 26 years, she turned to farming in the Eastern Cape of South Africa as a retirement project. She has a Stud Nguni herd of cattle.

Bobbie Troy maintains her sanity and perspective on life by writing flash fiction, poetry, and original fairy tales with a 21st century twist. Her work appears on line and in print at *Concise Delight Magazine of Short Poetry, vox poetica, SPARK, Haiku Ramblings, Caper Literary Journal, Leaf Garden Press, Journal of Liberal Arts and Education, Referential Magazine, Yes, Poetry, Cavalcade of Stars*, and *The Journal of Microliterature*. Her poem Dear Diane was nominated for a Pushcart Prize in 2009 and her fairy tale play Sasha and the Tree of Sorrows was produced in March 2011.

Marya Zilberberg is a health services researcher by day and a writer by night, but sometimes those hours overlap. Visit her blog: maryazilberberg.wordpress.com.

This collection comprises poems inspired by three photographs taken by Gianluca D'Elia, Annmarie Lockhart, and Patti Forehand and posted at the **prompts** page of **vox poetica** in the fall and winter of 2010. After appearing initially at **vox poetica**, prompts images and poems are only available in these *inspirations* collections.

vox poetica is an online literary salon dedicated to bringing poetry into the everyday. **vox poetica** accepts original submissions for publication at the **today's words** and **words to linger on** pages. Poems appearing at these site pages are archived at the **poemblog**.

Read ... write ... share ... be part of the expression experiment!

http://www.voxpoetica.com

www.ingramcontent.com/pod-product-compliance
Lightning Source LLC
Chambersburg PA
CBHW061357090426
42743CB00002B/43